CATS
& KITTENS
IN CROSS STITCH

CATS
& KITTENS
IN CROSS STITCH

JULIE HASLER

CASSELL

ACKNOWLEDGEMENTS

I would like to give my thanks to all the people who have
contributed a lot of time and effort in helping me with this book:
Stephanie Tihanyi for the original paintings from which these
designs have been produced; Steve Matthews for his help with
typing the manuscript; Allison Mortley, Barbara Hodgkinson,
Stella Baddeley, Odette Robinson, Jenny Whitlock, Joyce Formby,
Libby Shaw, Moira Walker, Diana Hewitt, Sue Dickinson and
Angela Clare Ferguson for sewing up the embroideries;
H. W. Peel & Co., Middlesex, for the graph paper; and Cara
Ackerman from DMC Creative World for the fabrics and silks.

This book is dedicated to my Mum

A CASSELL BOOK

First published in the UK 1992
by Cassell
Villiers House
41/47 Strand
London WC2N 5JE

Distributed in the United States
by Sterling Publishing Co., Inc.
387 Park Avenue South, New York, NY 10016-8810

Distributed in Australia
by Capricorn Link (Australia) Pty Ltd
P.O. Box 665, Lane Cove, NSW 2066

British Library Cataloguing in Publication Data

Hasler, Julie S.
    Cats and kittens in cross stitch.
    I. Title
    746.44

ISBN 0 304 34130 4 (*paperback*)
      0 304 34128 2 (*hardback*)

Typeset by MS Filmsetting Limited, Frome, Somerset
Printed in Hong Kong by Dah Hua Printing Press Co., Ltd.

Contents

———◆———

Introduction

————◆————

The favourite stitch of our great-grandmothers, cross stitch, is becoming increasingly popular in these modern times for the decoration of household furnishings, linen, children's clothes, in fact anything which lends itself to this type of embroidery; the possibilities are endless.

Cross stitch is one of the simplest, most versatile and elegant needlecrafts, and examples of its use can be found in many different countries and different eras.

The projects in this book make beautiful gifts for family and friends: gifts with a personal touch which have taken time and care to create, which will still be treasured long after shop-bought gifts have been forgotten.

Whether you are an experienced or inexperienced needleworker, you will be able to find projects in this book to suit your abilities. The designs can be worked by following the charts exactly or, by using your imagination, you can create your own designs by the use of alternative colours or by combining different motifs from several charts to create embroideries which are uniquely yours.

You will have to bear in mind that in counted thread work, the finished piece of work will not be the same size as the charted design unless the fabric you are working on has the same number of threads per inch as the chart has squares per inch.

General Guidance

—◆—

The designs in this book are created for counted cross stitch, a very enjoyable craft which you will find easy to learn — and inexpensive too!

The fabric you decide to sew your designs on and the number of strands of silk you use is your choice. You will find that the fabric is available in varying thread counts, and that there is a very wide choice of colours: white, ecru, pink, blue, lemon and pale green, to name but a few.

I chose 14-count Aida and 18-count Fine Aida in various colours to sew the designs in this book, using three strands of embroidery cotton for the cross stitch on the Aida, and two strands of embroidery cotton for those on the Fine Aida. Use your imagination to choose a fabric colour that will enhance your embroidery.

The charts are easy to read. Each square on the chart represents one stitch to be taken on the fabric, and each different symbol represents a different colour, the empty squares being background fabric. A colour key is given with each design.

If you wish to decorate clothing with any of the designs in this book, the most satisfactory method is to work the design over cross stitch fabric basted to the clothing material and remove the cross stitch fabric afterwards, thread by thread. This will leave the cross stitch embroidery on the clothing material beneath.

Relax, enjoy sewing the designs, and make something beautiful for you and your home!

Techniques

—◆—

CROSS STITCH

To begin: bring the thread through at the lower right-hand side, leaving a short length of thread on the underside of the work and anchoring it with the first few stitches as in Figs 1 and 2. Insert the needle across the mesh into the next hole above and diagonally to the left and bring it out through the hole across the mesh but immediately below. Half the stitch is now completed.

Continue in the same way to the end of the row. Your stitches should be diagonal on the right side of the fabric and vertical on the wrong side. Complete the upper half of the stitch by returning in the opposite direction, as in Fig. 3.

Cross stitch can be worked in either direction, from right to left or left to right, but it is of the utmost importance that the upper half of each cross lies in the same direction.

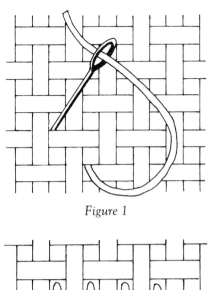

Figure 1

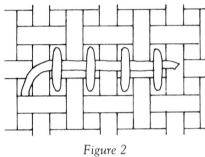

Figure 2

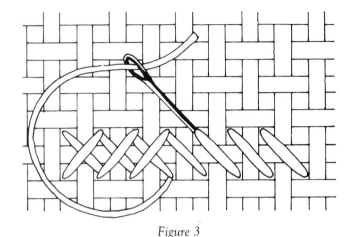

Figure 3

BACKSTITCH

Backstitch is used in many of the designs, mainly for outlines and finer details, as shown in the keys. Work any backstitch when your cross stitch embroidery has been completed. Always use one strand less of yarn than that used for the cross stitch embroidery. For example, if three strands of stranded cotton have been used to work the cross stitch embroidery, use two strands for the backstitching. If two strands of stranded cotton were used to work the cross stitch embroidery, one strand is used for the backstitching.

Backstitch is worked from hole to hole and can be stitched as a horizontal, diagonal or vertical line, as shown in Fig. 4. Always take care not to pull the stitches too tight, otherwise the contrast of colour will be lost against the cross stitches. Finish off the threads as for cross stitch.

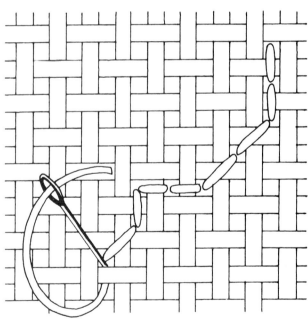

Figure 4

Materials

—— ◆ ——

NEEDLES
A small blunt tapestry needle, no. 24 or 26, is best for cross stitch.

SCISSORS
A sharp pair of embroidery scissors is essential, especially if a mistake has to be removed.

EMBROIDERY HOOP
A round plastic or wooden hoop with a screw-type tension adjuster, 4, 5 or 6 in (10, 13 or 15 cm) in diameter, is ideal for cross stitch. Place the area of fabric to be embroidered over the inner ring and gently push the outer ring over it, ensuring that the fabric is taut and the mesh straight, and gradually tighten the screw adjuster.

THREADS
DMC six-strand embroidery cotton has been used to colour-code the designs in this book. The number of strands used will depend on the fabric you decide to work on.

FABRIC
Do not choose a fabric which does not have an even weave, as this will distort the design either vertically or horizontally. An evenweave fabric on which it is easy to count the threads should be used. There is a variety on the market to choose from in varying thread counts and colours. The most popular fabrics used are Aida cloth and Hardanger cloth.

Cotton Aida is available in the following sizes: 8, 11, 14 and 18 threads per inch, and is known as Fine Aida.

Linen is available in the following sizes: 19/20, 25/26 and 30/31 threads per inch.

Hardanger is 22 threads per inch.

Preparing to Work

—— ◆ ——

To determine the size of the finished embroidery, count the squares on the chart for the entire width and depth of the design, and divide each by the number of threads per inch in the fabric you intend to use. This will give the dimensions in inches. Cut the fabric at least 2 in (5 cm) wider each way than the size of the design to allow for finishing. To prevent the fabric from fraying, either machine-stitch or whip-stitch the outer edges or alternatively bind them with masking tape.

Find the centre of the fabric by folding it in half vertically and then horizontally. Mark the centre with a line of basting stitches both lengthwise and widthwise. All the charts in this book have arrows marking the vertical and horizontal centres. Follow these arrows to their intersection to locate the centre of the chart.

It is preferable to begin cross stitch at the top of the design. To find the top, count the squares up from the centre of the chart and then the number of holes up from the centre of the fabric. Ensure that the fabric is held tautly in the embroidery hoop, as this makes stitching easier, enabling the needle to be pushed through the holes without piercing the fibres of the fabric. If the fabric loosens while you work, retighten as necessary. When working, you will find it easier to have the screw in the ten o'clock position to prevent your thread from becoming tangled in it with each stitch. If you are left-handed, have the screw in the one o'clock position.

When working with stranded cotton, always separate the strands before threading the needle. This will give better coverage of the fabric. The number of strands will depend on the fabric count that you use.

Useful Tips

———◆———

1 When you are stitching, it is important not to pull the fabric out of shape. You can accomplish this by working the stitches in two motions, straight up through a hole in the fabric and then straight down, ensuring that the fabric remains taut. Make sure that you don't pull the thread tight — snug, but not tight. If you use this method, you will find that the thread will lie just where you want it to and not pull your fabric out of shape.

2 If your thread becomes twisted while working, drop your needle and let it hang down freely. It will then untwist itself. Do not continue working with twisted thread as it will appear thinner and not cover your fabric as well.

3 Never leave your needle in the design area of your work when not in use. No matter how good the needle might be, it could rust in time and mark your work permanently.

4 Do not carry thread across the back of an open expanse of fabric. If you are working separate areas of the same colour, finish off and begin again. Loose threads, especially dark colours, will be visible from the right side of your work when the project is completed.

Finishing

———◆———

When the embroidery is finished, it will need to be pressed. Place the finished work right side down on your ironing board, cover it with a thin, slightly dampened cloth, and iron.

If you intend to frame the finished embroidery yourself, you will need to block it. Cut a piece of board to the desired size and place the finished embroidery over it. Fold the surplus fabric to the back and secure along the top edge of the board with pins. Pull firmly over the opposite edge and pin in position.

Repeat this procedure along both side edges, pulling the fabric until it is lying taut on the board.

Secure at the back by lacing from side to side on all four sides with strong thread. Remove the pins. Your embroidery picture is now ready to be framed. The best result will be achieved if you take it to a professional framer. If you want a glazed frame, the effect will be improved by using non-reflective glass. Although it is slightly more expensive, it is well worth it.

After-care of your Cross Stitch Embroideries

You may find at some stage that your cross stitch projects will need to be laundered. This is no problem: just follow the simple advice supplied by DMC in conjunction with their six-stranded cotton. The following recommendations are for washing embroidery separately from all other laundry.

	COTTON OR LINEN FABRIC	SYNTHETIC FABRIC
RECOMMENDED WASHING	Wash in warm soapy water. Rinse thoroughly. Squeeze without twisting and hang to dry. Iron on reverse side using two layers of white linen.	Not recommended.
BLEACHING OR WHITENING AGENT	Product should be diluted according to manufacturer's instructions. The embroidery should be pre-soaked in clear water first, then soaked for 5 minutes in a solution of about 1 tablespoon of bleaching agent to 1 quart (4·5 l) of cold water. Rinse thoroughly in cold water.	The same instructions are recommended if the white of the fabric is not of a high standard. If the fabric is a pure white (white with a bluish tinge) do not use bleaching or whitening agent.
DRY CLEANING	Avoid dry cleaning. Some spot removers (benzine, trichlorethylene) can be used for an occasional small stain.	Not recommended, even for occasional small stains.

My Love of Cats

———◆———

My love of cats began at the very early age of five, whilst I was returning from a summer holiday in Broadstairs, Kent. My parents stopped off at a farm to buy a sack of potatoes. As we approached the farmhouse, we heard the sound of mewing from a nearby barn. Looking over, we saw a row of tiny kittens' heads peering from underneath the barn door. They were so sweet that my mother asked if we could see them. A farm-worker showed us into the barn, and told us that the mother was a stray, living wild off the land, who had come to the barn to have her kittens. Although they had been feeding the mother while she was caring for the kittens, he told us that they had to get rid of them soon, as they were causing a nuisance.

Being very concerned about this, my mother told me to choose one to take home. I picked the prettiest one of the litter, a female long-haired tortoiseshell that we later named Puskin. As an adult cat, she behaved more like a dog by nature, accompanying my father and me for miles on our nightly walks across the fields and woods at the back of our house. She even came to meet me from school most days, waiting about half a mile from home. However, she never seemed to lose her original wild instincts. She was a very keen hunter, forever bringing home birds, rabbits, rats, mice and many other delightful presents from the fields.

She was a very temperamental and often vicious cat, soon letting you know if she didn't want to be made a fuss of by jumping at your arm, digging all her claws in and kicking with her back feet. A painful and unpleasant experience, but to a child most amusing when an unsuspecting relative falls victim.

We had Puskin for twelve years, until, sadly, she died from kidney failure. I missed her so much when she died, that within a few days, I felt I had to get another cat. I tried absolutely everywhere to find a kitten. Animal shelters, advertisements in local papers, newsagents' windows, all to no avail. Everyone told me that it was the wrong time of year for kittens, but if I could wait a month or so. . . .

I couldn't. Not even a week or so. In desperation, I phoned the local vet to see if any kittens or young cats had been brought in. I was told they had had a stray brought in that morning — a black-and-white tom-cat. My heart sank. How ordinary, I thought. I really wanted another tortoiseshell or a long-haired female cat of some description. Then the vet told me that if they couldn't find a home for it, the cat would have to be put down the next day. I told him I would come down to see it. I jumped into my car, repeatedly telling myself not just to grab any cat for the sake of trying to replace Puskin, and drove down to the surgery. The tom-cat was in a very sorry state. Scruffy, with dirty long fur and covered in fleas and ticks. When the vet handed him to me, he put his paws either side of my neck, looked at me and began purring very loudly. What could I do? I just had to have him. I thought he was gorgeous.

We definitely needed each other. I handed him back to the vet, asked him to get rid of his fleas and ticks and neuter him, and said I would pick him up the next day.

This cat was to be called Elvis. He was about two years old according to the vet, and he had a lovely temperament. Very affectionate and homely, he became a real lap-cat. Perhaps he was just glad to have found a loving family. Elvis endured three house moves with me, never trying very hard to get on with the neighbours' cats — he was a bit of a bully. Around me, however, he was different: a very attention-seeking cat. I remember one time when he had been limping very badly and kept on coming up to me and showing me one of his front paws. Seeing nothing wrong with it, I thought it couldn't be very important but after a week of seeing him limp around looking sorry for himself, and eventually not using this front paw at all but managing on three legs, I took him to the vet. I put him on the table in the surgery, explained the problem, and let go of Elvis, who proceeded to jump down off the table and run around the room (using all four legs) like a maniac. The vet gave me a rather quizzical look, caught Elvis, examined his 'bad' leg and informed me that there was absolutely nothing wrong with it. Apparently, he was doing it to gain more attention! Rather red-faced, I beat a hasty retreat, cat under arm, and

went home. Elvis never limped again. Very strange.

I had Elvis quite a few years until he was about eight, when unfortunately his bad road-sense got the better of him and he managed to get himself knocked down by a milk float.

After Elvis, a string of cats came and went. Scruffy was another stray, a pedigree Chinchilla. She came to me in a terrible state and had to have most of her fur shaved off as it was so matted. She too was covered in fleas and had open sores on her tummy. After about six months all her fur had grown back and she looked really beautiful. Chico and Zoe were litter-mates I had from kittens; they were black-and-white semi-long-coated. Lema was a black-and-ginger short-hair, and had a litter of four kittens which I found good homes for.

I just have Chico left now, but I must say he has been my favourite. He has a lovely gentle personality, rather like a Ragdoll cat. I think this came about by his unusual upbringing. When he was a kitten, I used to take him everywhere with me. Around the house he would either sit on my shoulder or cling to the front of my jumper wherever I went. When I visited the local shops, I would take him with me and put him in the shopping basket, or sit him by the till while I shopped. He even used to enjoy coming out in the car. When he grew into an adult cat, this became impractical, but he still sits with me nearly all day and loves being carried about upside-down, which most cats will not tolerate. He is very gentle and never bites or scratches anyone. He is eight years old now, still in good health and spoiled rotten. He has his own chairs in the house, and sleeps in the linen basket beside my bed every night.

Having these cats seemed to trigger off some sort of obsession within me. My house is now full of cat things. Every room you enter has a cat somewhere. Framed pictures include watercolours, prints, needlepoint and cross stitch designs. I have a reproduction enamel advertisement for Black Cat cigarettes, cat cushions, over thirty books on cats, some bought just for the pleasing illustrations, a ceramic cat lamp and a collection of over fifty cat ornaments.

My favourite cat item must be a gold charm which I bought at an antique fair years ago. I wear it as an earring.

This obsession with cats inspired me to design my first needlepoint picture and eventually, in 1986, my first book of cat and kitten designs was published. I have had many charted design books published since then, but I felt it was time to write another cat book.

I know that if you love cats as much as I do, you will enjoy *Cats and Kittens in Cross Stitch*. I just hope you have as much fun making the projects as I did in designing them and writing the book.

Elegance

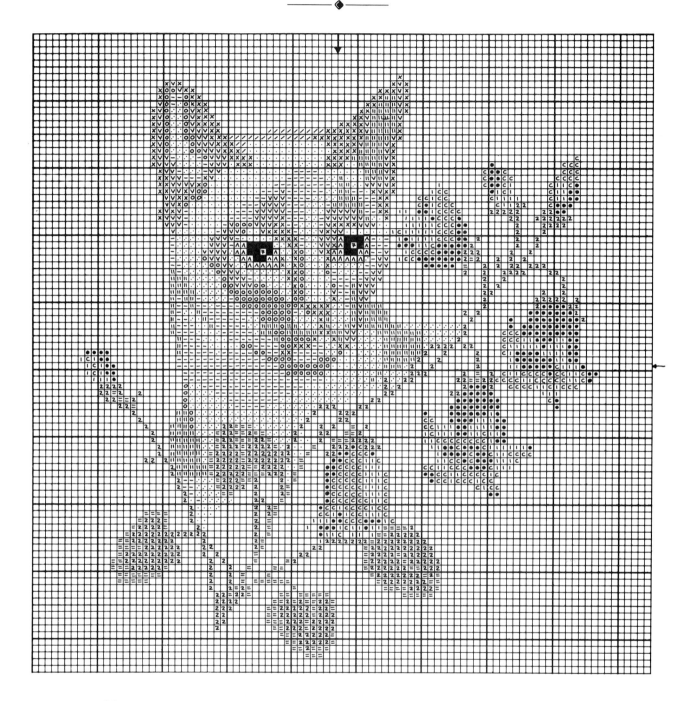

⊡ 746 off-white	⊞ 729 medium old gold	□ 341 light lilac
■ 310 black and outline eyes	⊙ 832 golden wheat yellow	c 340 periwinkle blue
7 white	⊡ 3047 pale golden wheat	2 503 blue green
⊘ 676 light old gold	⊟ 3046 golden wheat	= 501 dark blue green
⊠ 829 dark avocado leaf brown	● 333 dark lilac	⋀ 794 pale blue
⊻ 831 light avocado leaf brown		

Surprise

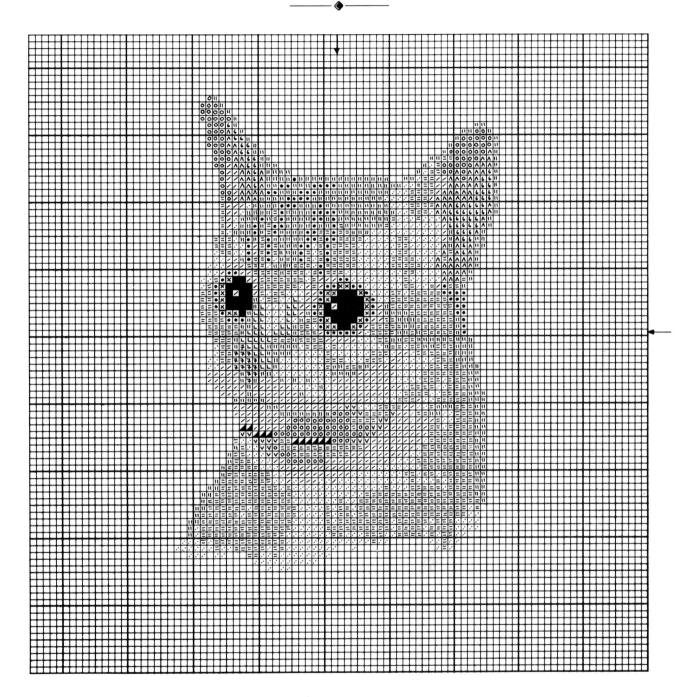

☒ 725 topaz yellow	⊙ 415 pale grey	⋀ 948 very light peach	
■ 310 black and outline eyes	‖ 3045 dark golden wheat	ʕ 353 peach	
⧄ white	◤ 318 light steel grey	Ⅼ 754 light peach	
⋯ 677 very light old gold	⋁ 762 very light pearl grey	₮ 352 medium peach	
⦿ 610 very dark drab brown	＝ 422 golden beige		

Tabby Cat with Roses

☒	353 peach	⁷	722 pale orange
②	605 very light cranberry	⌐	502 medium blue green
◉	350 light red	⁴	504 light blue green
☑	351 dark peach	③	503 blue green
ᵋ	352 medium peach	◪	501 dark blue green
Ⓒ	822 light beige grey	L	743 dark yellow
⫿	524 light olive drab green	T	744 medium yellow
⊟	white	·	745 light yellow
◿	3047 pale golden wheat	H	741 medium tangerine orange
⊜	422 golden beige	ⓨ	223 dark antique pink
⫼	3045 dark golden wheat	⦀	761 light salmon red
◼	3031 very dark brown	☰	754 light peach
⊞	522 olive drab green	⑧	801 dark coffee brown
⋀	435 very light brown	⊙	642 beige grey
◣	611 dark drab brown	◺	3032 medium beige
⊙	758 pale brick red	F	368 light pistachio green
◁	613 light drab brown	◫	310 black and outline eyes
⋰	963 very light dusty rose pink		

Photo on p. 20

TABBY CAT WITH ROSES
See pp.18–19

YOUNG KITTEN IN THE GARDEN
See pp.22-3

Young Kitten in the Garden

■ 310 black and outline eyes	⊞ 780 very dark topaz brown
☒ white	▥ 830 avocado leaf brown
⧄ 611 dark drab brown	⌈ 355 brick red
⊡ 746 off white	V 606 bright orange red
‖ 738 very light tan	7 977 golden brown
○ 422 golden beige	⌉ 975 dark golden brown
◪ 224 antique pink	C 3348 light yellow green
⁘ 739 fawn beige	⧅ 3346 dark yellow green
2 725 topaz yellow	⊜ 907 light parrot green
∧ 782 medium topaz brown	4 906 medium parrot green

Photo on p. 21

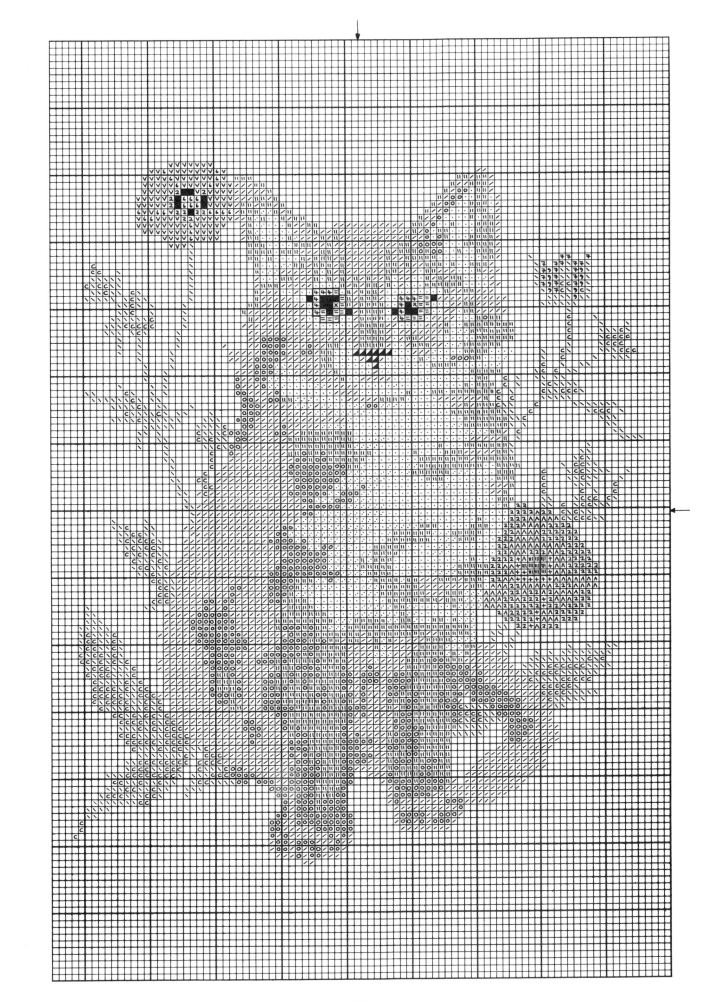

Contentment

◆

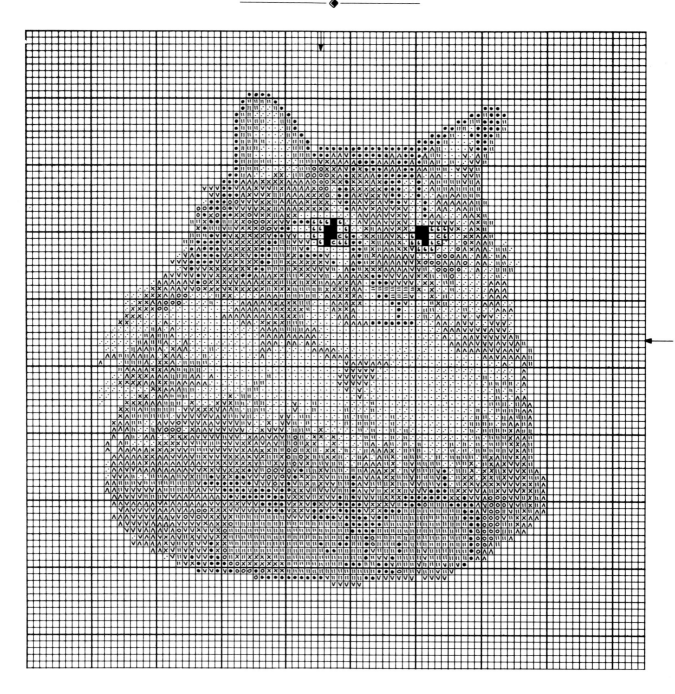

⸍	783 christmas gold	⋅	white	⸍⸍	739 fawn beige
C	725 topaz yellow	●	801 dark coffee brown	V	433 medium brown
≡	353 peach	■	310 black and outline eyes	⊙	434 light brown
‖	437 light tan brown	⊠	436 tan brown	∧	738 very light brown

CONTENTMENT

Tabby Cat on a Window-sill

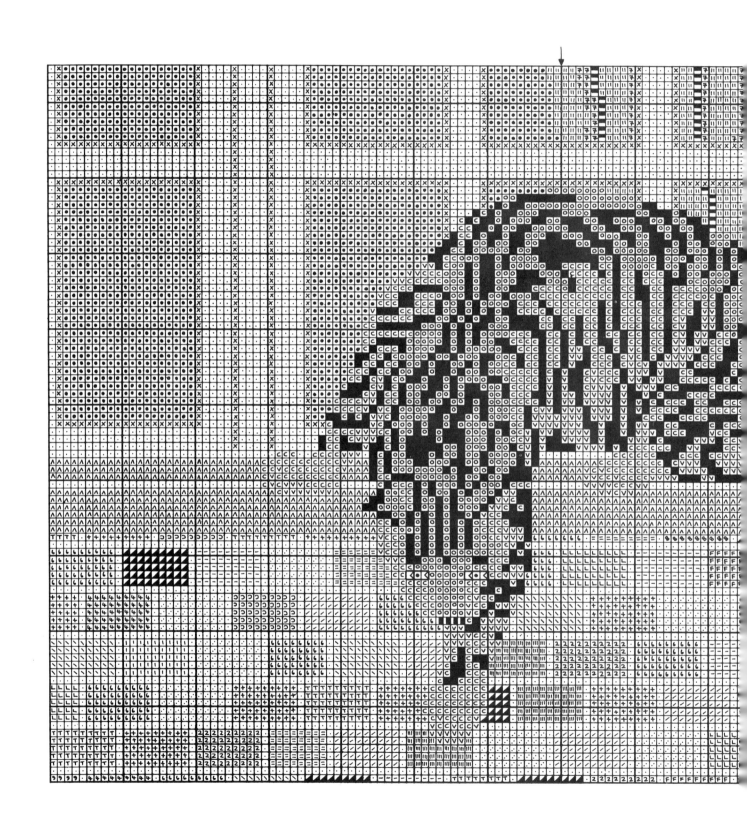

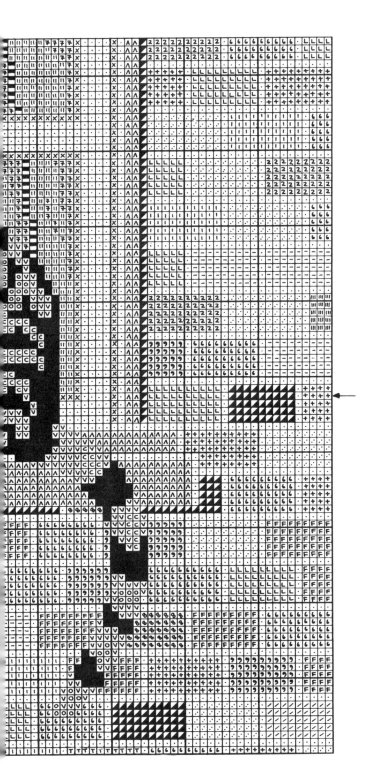

■	3021 very dark brown grey	▯	3046 golden wheat
V	612 drab brown	2	613 light drab brown
c	739 fawn beige	•	927 antique blue
○	437 light tan brown	▢	3045 dark golden wheat
●	310 black and outline eyes	–	452 medium shell grey
·	white	=	3032 medium beige
X	3072 very light beaver grey	4	422 golden beige
◿	758 pale brick red	◿	834 light golden wheat yellow
‖	352 medium peach	◥	3012 medium khaki green
7	353 peach	⫴	503 blue green
◖	350 light red	F	372 golden khaki
Λ	415 pale grey	◁	725 topaz yellow
◢	318 light steel grey	L	642 beige grey
T	402 very light mahogany brown	,	640 dark beige grey
+	3042 light antique lilac	8	3022 brown grey
·	648 light beaver grey	◨	761 light salmon red

Photo on pp. 28–9

· 27 ·

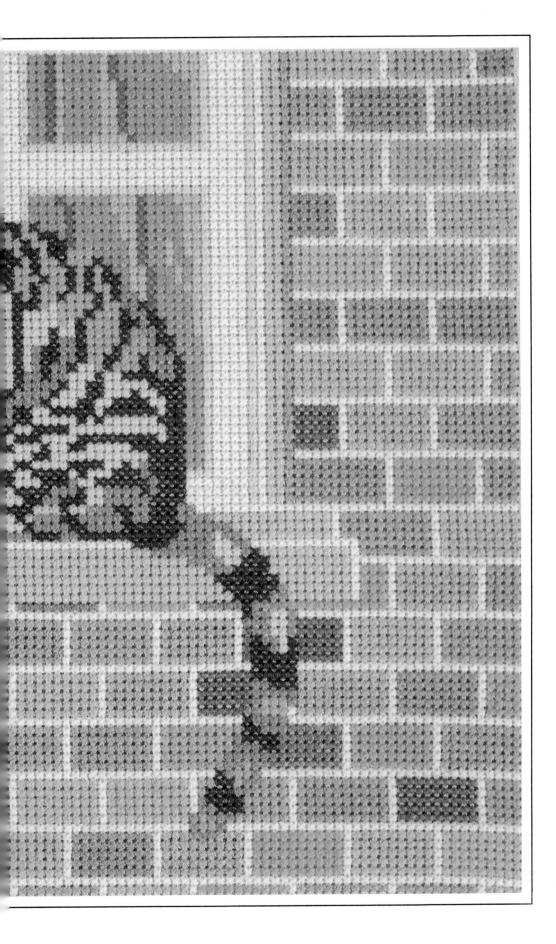

TABBY CAT ON
A WINDOW-SILL
See pp.26–7

Tabby Kitten with a Toy Mouse

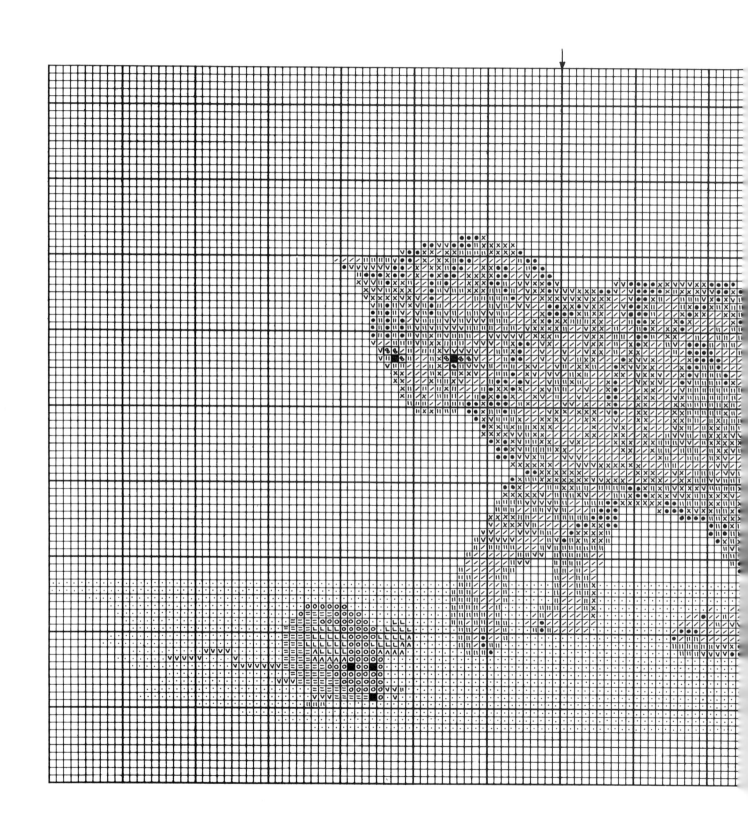

●	413 very dark steel grey
✕	317 medium steel grey
∨	318 light steel grey
‖	415 pale grey
╱	762 very light pearl grey
■	310 black and outline eyes
⑧	3348 light yellow green
○	739 fawn beige
☰	738 very light tan
∧	754 light peach
L	352 medium peach
•	911 medium emerald green

Maine Coon Cat with Blackberries

———◆———

⊡	white	⊟	422	golden beige
⊡	739 fawn beige	⊘	3045	dark golden wheat
⊡	738 very light tan	⑧	725	topaz yellow
⋁	414 steel grey	F	783	christmas gold
⊙	318 light steel grey	C	3346	dark yellow green
‖	415 pale grey	⊠	3348	light yellow green
⊟	762 very light pearl grey	■	310	black and outline eyes
⬤	610 very dark drab brown	Z	758	pale brick red
⋀	611 dark drab brown	◢	939	very dark navy blue
7	3047 pale golden wheat	⌐	3328	medium salmon red

Black-and-white Cat
in the Garden

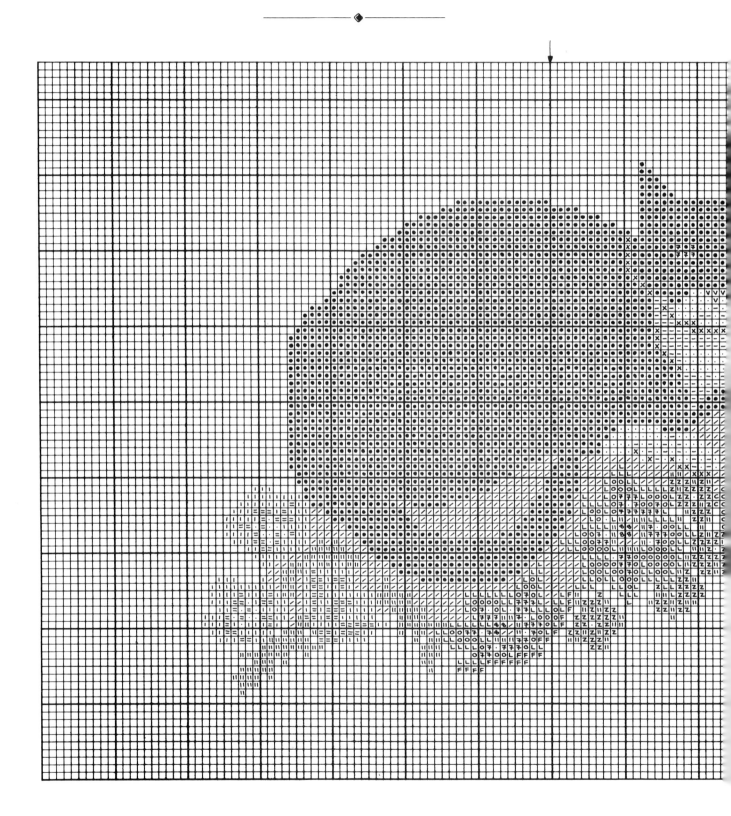

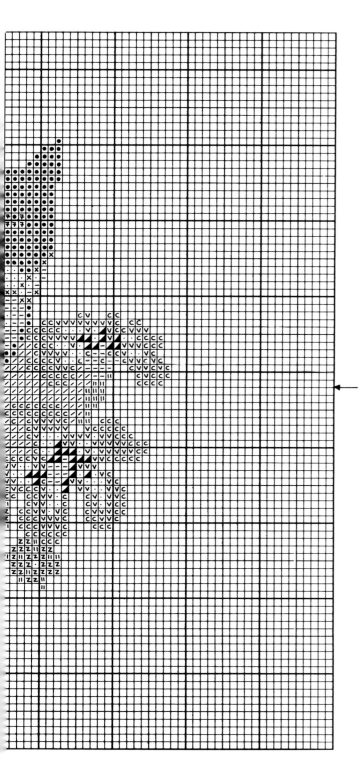

- ● 310 black
- ⊠ 414 steel grey
- ⊟ 415 pale grey
- · white
- ⧄ 989 light forest green
- ‖ 987 dark forest green
- ₣ 725 topaz yellow
- ⊺ 825 dark blue
- ⊜ 813 light blue

- Z 826 medium blue
- C 3328 medium salmon red
- V 761 light salmon red
- ◤ 794 pale blue
- L 776 medium baby pink
- O 335 dark pink
- 8 472 very light avocado green
- F 326 very deep rose red

Tabby-and-white

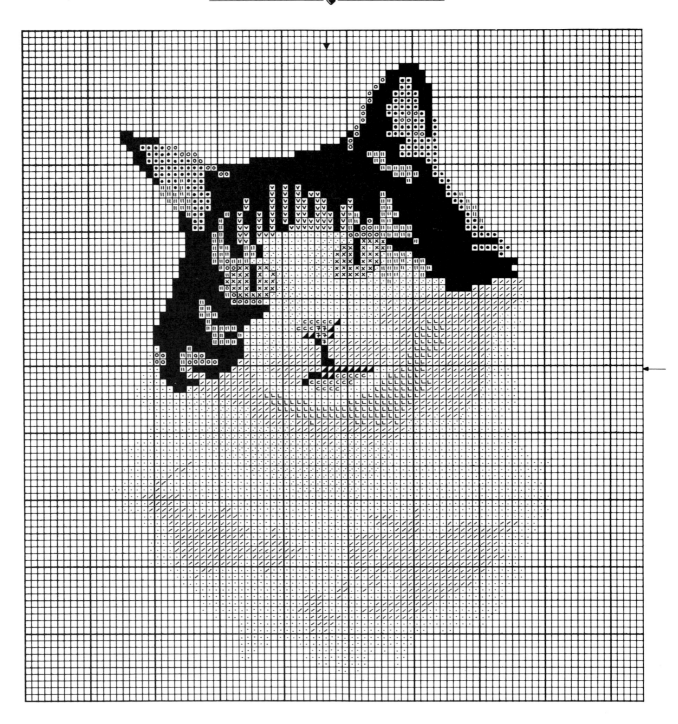

■ 310 black and outline eyes	▨ 415 pale grey	⊡ 353 peach
⊠ 3348 light yellow green	⊙ 436 tan brown	⊡ 352 medium peach
⊙ 801 dark coffee brown	∨ 738 very light tan	· white
⸭ 762 very light pearl grey	⊔ 414 steel grey	◪ 413 very dark steel grey
⊪ 433 medium brown		

TABBY-AND-WHITE

White Turkish Angora Kitten

◆

▥	221	claret
☒	754	light peach
⊡		white
⊡	762	very light pearl grey
◺	415	pale grey
◉	318	light steel grey
◪	414	steel grey and outline mouth
◎	809	delft blue
☑	948	very light peach
■	310	black and outline eyes

Photo on p. 40

WHITE TURKISH ANGORA KITTEN
See pp.38–9

TABBY CAT WITH SCARLET FLAX
See pp.42–3

Tabby Cat with Scarlet Flax

◆

F	3064 spice brown	C	309 deep rose red
I	762 very light pearl grey	··	899 medium pink
◁	415 pale grey	V	470 medium avocado green
'	414 steel grey	●	472 very light avocado green
=	310 black	◥	471 light avocado green
X	436 tan brown	2	3032 medium beige
L	738 very light tan	◢	814 dark garnet red
T	612 drab brown	○	644 medium beige grey
4	353 peach	◿	611 dark drab brown
·	white	■	938 dark forest brown
Λ	937 dark avocado green	II	437 light tan brown

Photo on p. 41

Blue Persian with Peruvian Lilies

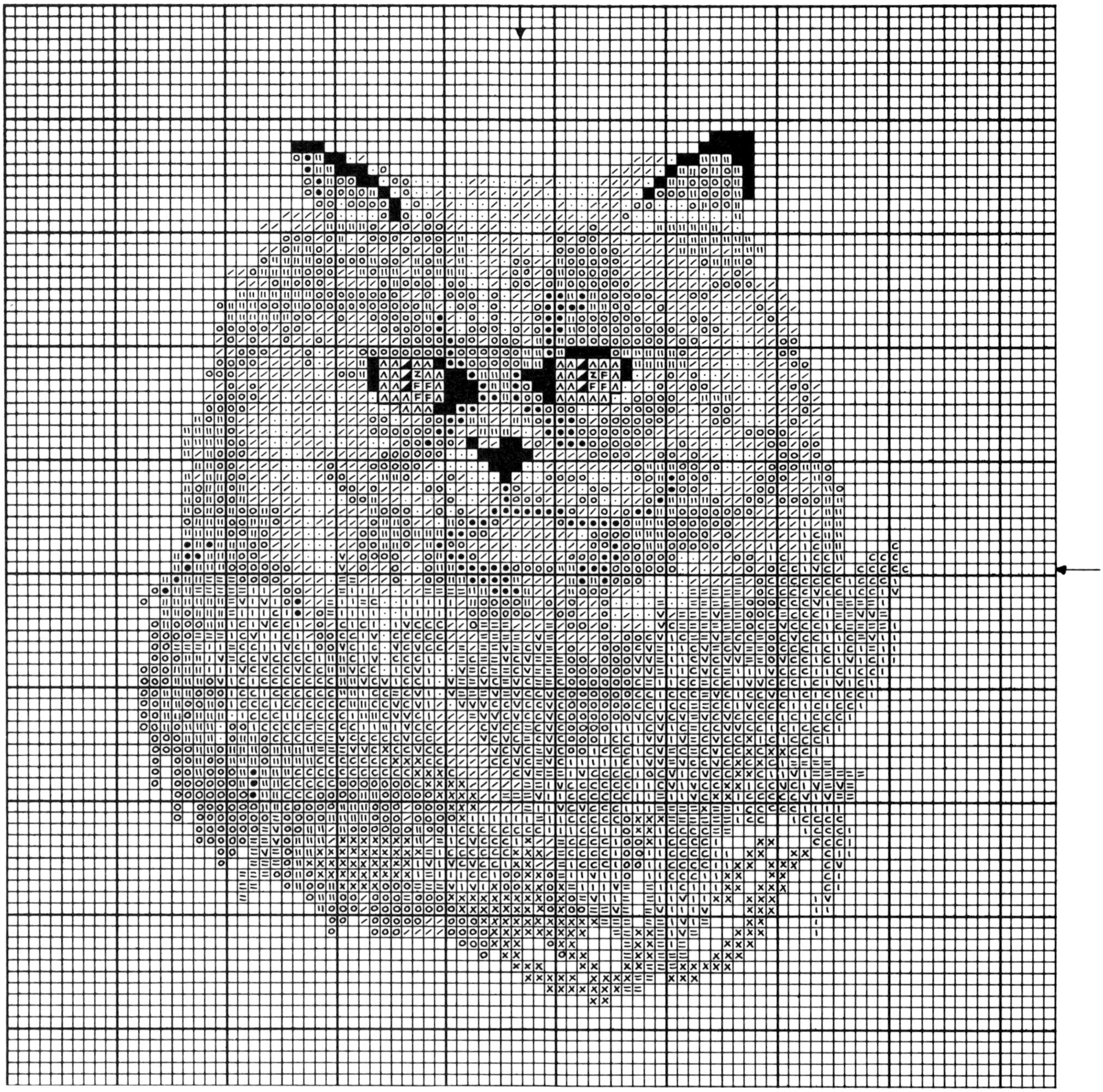

- ■ 413 very dark steel grey
- ● 317 medium steel grey
- · 762 very light pearl grey
- || 414 steel grey
- ○ 318 light steel grey
- / 415 pale grey
- ◢ 310 black and outline eyes
- Z white
- X 913 medium nile green
- V 975 dark golden brown
- ≡ 976 medium golden brown
- I 977 golden brown
- C 725 topaz yellow
- ^ 729 medium old gold
- F 676 light old gold

BLUE PERSIAN WITH PERUVIAN LILIES

Superiority

———◆———

●	975 dark golden brown	C	435 very light brown
×	976 medium golden brown	Z	840 beige brown
=	898 very dark coffee brown	╱	415 pale grey
○	977 golden brown	+	318 light steel grey
∴	739 fawn beige	Ⅲ	317 medium steel grey
‖	738 very light tan	◣	760 salmon red
L	437 light tan brown	◖	347 dark salmon red
∨	436 tan brown	◢	725 topaz yellow
■	310 black and outline eyes	‖	472 very light avocado green
·	white	=	470 medium avocado green
∧	758 pale brick red	8	800 pale delft blue

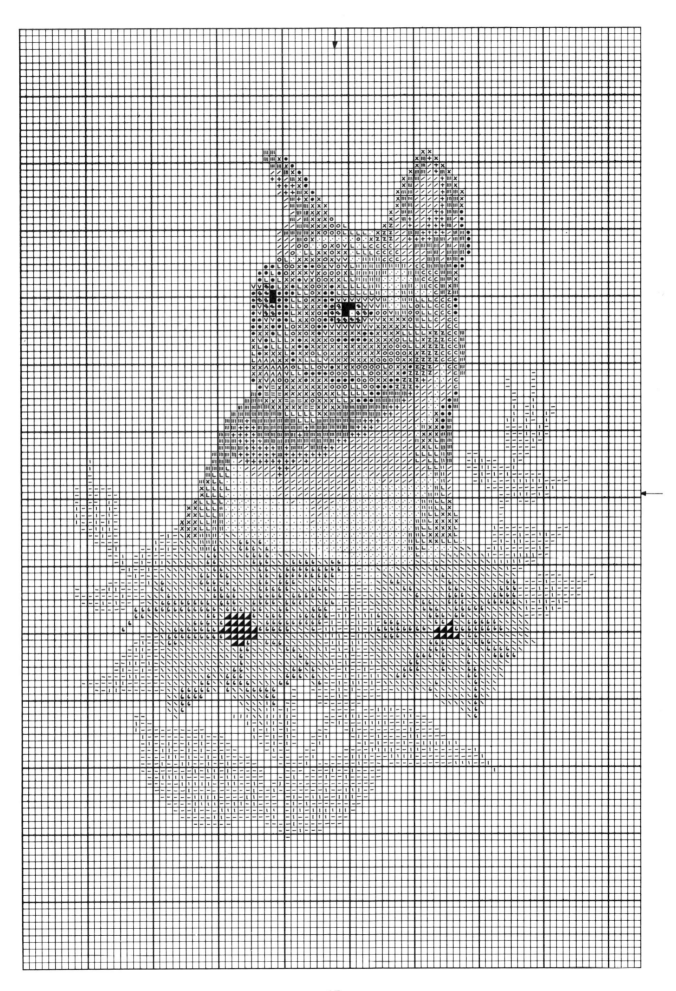

Long-haired Kitten with Wild Roses

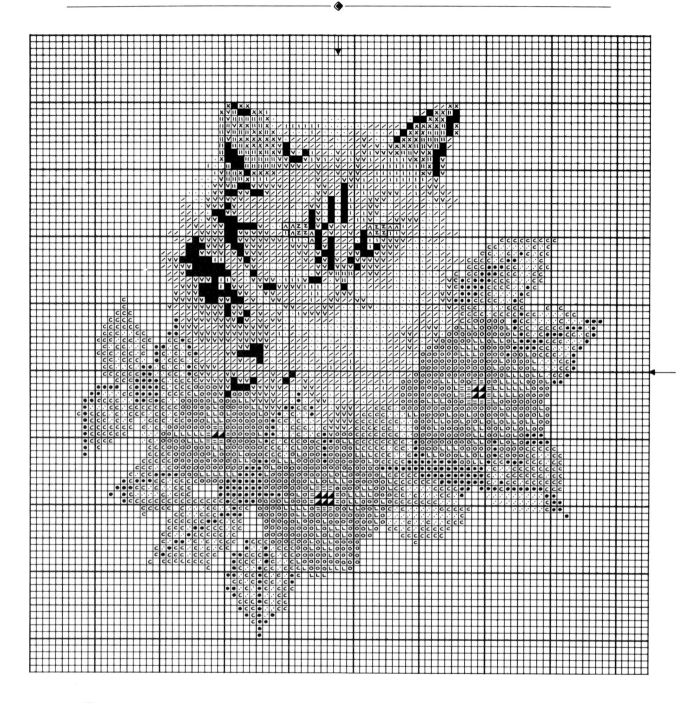

·	822 light beige grey	‖	353 peach	∴	369 very light pistachio green
I	644 medium beige grey	O	899 medium pink	=	742 light tangerine orange
■	317 medium steel grey	L	776 medium baby pink	◪	733 khaki
V	318 light steel grey	●	319 dark green	Z	310 black and outline eyes
╱	415 pale grey	C	320 medium pistachio green	∧	977 golden brown
X	948 very light peach				

First Exploration

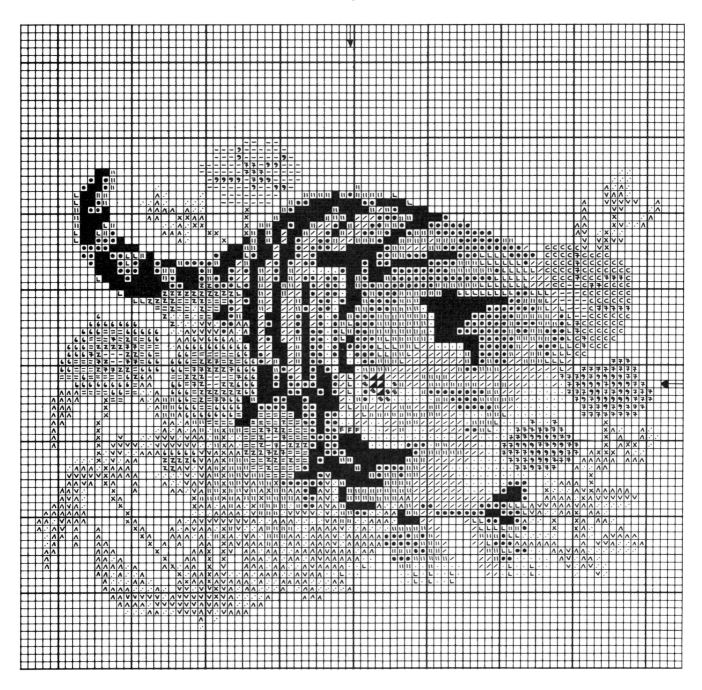

◤ 310 black	⌷ 647 medium beaver grey	﹃ 920 medium copper	⊂ 726 light topaz yellow
⋅ white	‖ 646 beaver grey	Z 326 very deep rose red	✕ 356 medium brick red
⑧ 800 pale delft blue	● 645 dark beaver grey	⊟ 335 dark pink	∨ 319 dark green
F 353 peach	■ 844 very dark beaver grey	⊂ 3326 pink	∧ 320 medium pistachio green
⟋ 648 light beaver grey	﹃ 742 light tangerine orange	⊟ 970 light pumpkin orange	⋰ 369 very light pistachio green

Grey Tabby with Cushions

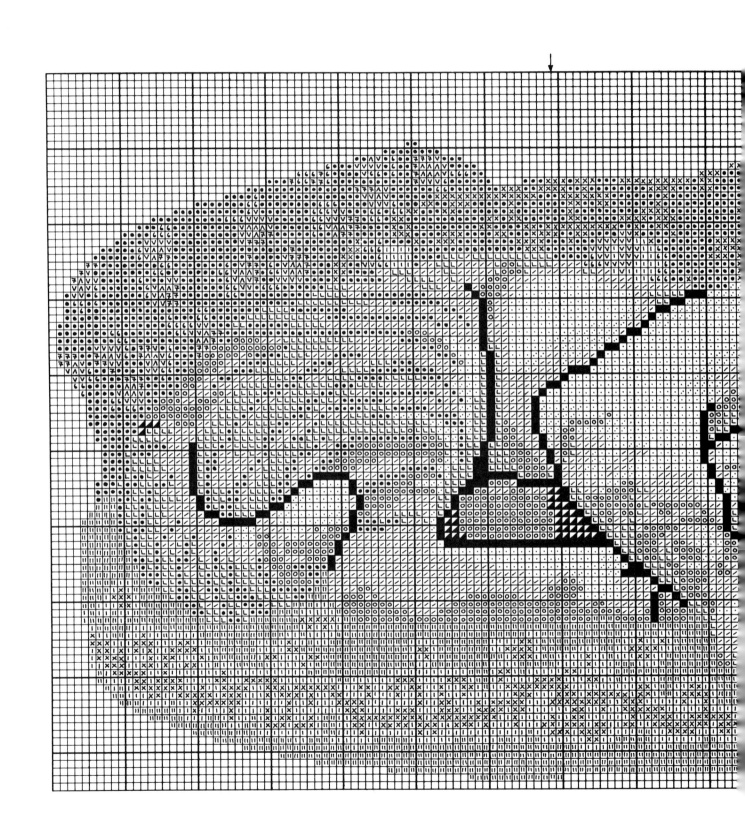

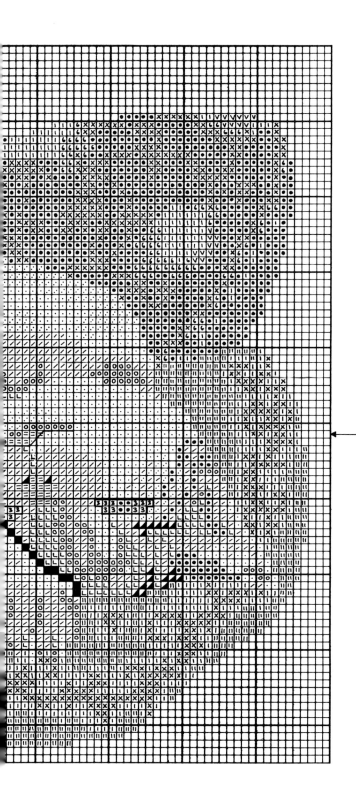

7	741	medium tangerine orange
∧	899	medium pink
‖	938	dark forest brown
∨	209	dark lavender
Ⅰ	309	deep rose red
●	310	black and outline on cat's face
ᴄ	912	light emerald green
✕	783	christmas gold
■	413	very dark steel grey
∴	762	very light pearl grey
·		white
∕	415	pale grey
○	318	light steel grey
L	414	steel grey
◢	317	medium steel grey
3	3348	light yellow green
=	761	light salmon red

Photo on pp. 52–3

GREY TABBY WITH
CUSHIONS
See pp.50–1

Black-and-white Tom-cat with Flowers

———◆———

- ■ 310 black and outline eyes
- ◉ 413 very dark steel grey
- ⊠ 318 light steel grey
- ▱ 415 pale grey
- · white
- ⊻ 754 light peach
- ② 352 medium peach
- ‖ 987 dark forest green
- © 989 light forest green
- ⌶ 369 very light pistachio green
- ⊙ 350 light red
- ⋀ 3348 light yellow green

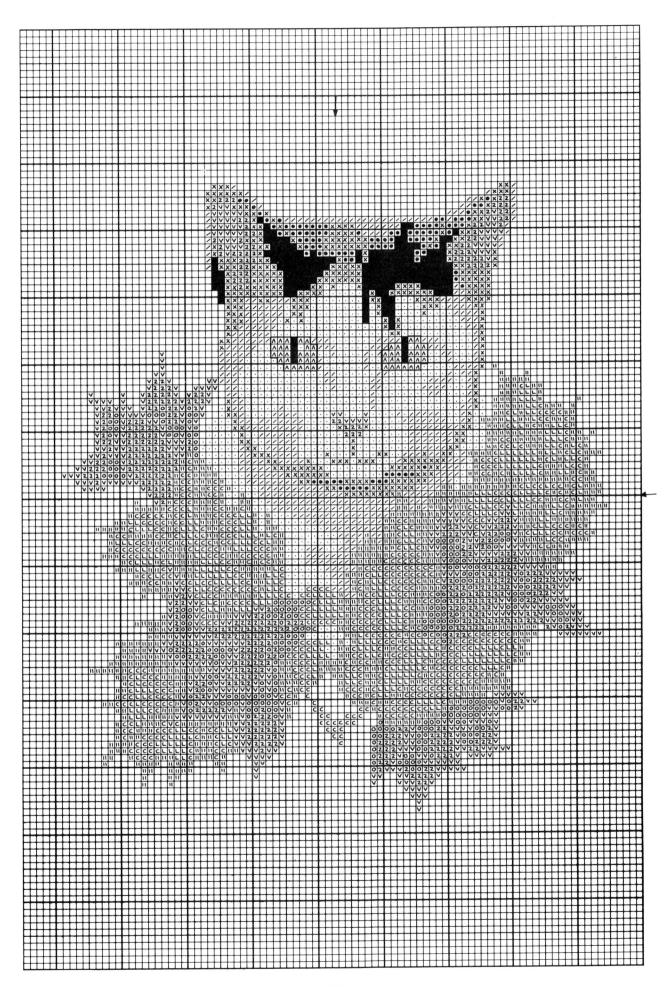

Buster

—◆—

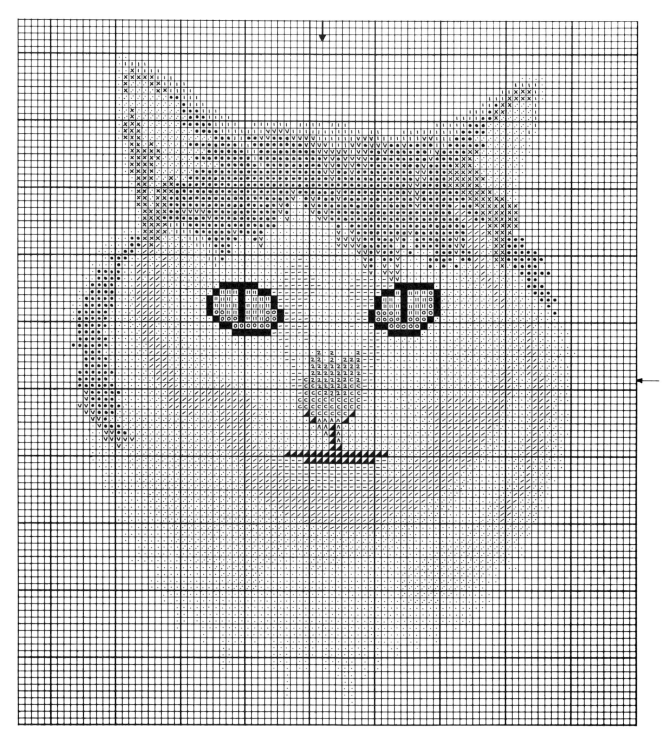

⊡	white	☑	976 medium golden brown	⊟	762 very light pearl grey
⊞	977 golden brown	◪	318 light steel grey	©	754 light peach
☒	414 steel grey	■	310 black	②	948 very light peach
⊡	415 pale grey	⊞	471 light avocado green	◪	317 medium steel grey
●	975 dark golden brown	⊙	472 very light avocado green	⋀	353 peach

BUSTER

Burmese Cat with Flowers

T	783 christmas gold	7	3689 light mauve
≡	975 dark golden brown	⊃	3688 medium mauve
◁	976 medium golden brown	≣	3687 mauve
H	415 pale grey	⊔	550 very dark violet
y	762 very light pearl grey	⅃	554 light violet
3	611 dark drab brown	∧	725 topaz yellow
2	3325 baby blue	8	727 very light topaz yellow
◪	322 dark baby blue	‹	726 light topaz yellow
·	white	∴	3348 light yellow green
●	3371 very dark forest brown and outline eyes	C	989 light forest green
‖	644 medium beige grey	◧	986 very dark forest green
+	613 light drab brown	∨	326 very deep rose red
×	610 very dark drab brown	⊓	899 medium pink
■	310 black	⊟	335 dark pink
⦀	3685 dark mauve	L	422 golden beige

Photo on p. 60

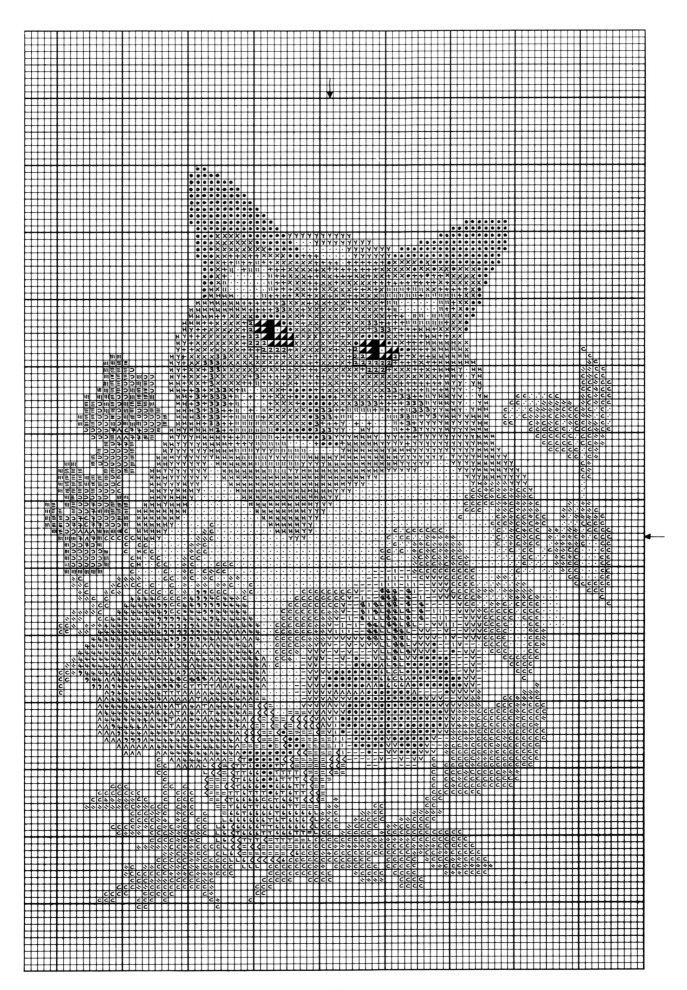

BURMESE CAT WITH FLOWERS
See pp.58–9

· OPPOSITE ·
BLUE PERSIAN WITH QUILT AND PILLOWS
See pp.62–3

Blue Persian with Quilt and Pillows

◆

⊙	989 light forest green	7	744 medium yellow
⊘	758 pale brick red	∧	743 dark yellow
‖	799 medium delft blue	⊃	754 light peach
⊟	899 medium pink	⫴	742 light tangerine orange
◲	3326 pink	⸜	335 dark pink
∨	977 golden brown	⸞	776 medium baby pink
⸍	350 light red	⊠	720 dark orange
⊂	800 pale delft blue	2	725 topaz yellow
■	413 very dark steel grey and outline eyes	◁	783 christmas gold
◩	310 black	⊓	white
⊡	415 pale grey	⊔	317 medium steel grey
⊙	326 very deep rose red	◳	318 light steel grey

Photo on p. 61

Ginger-and-white Short-hair

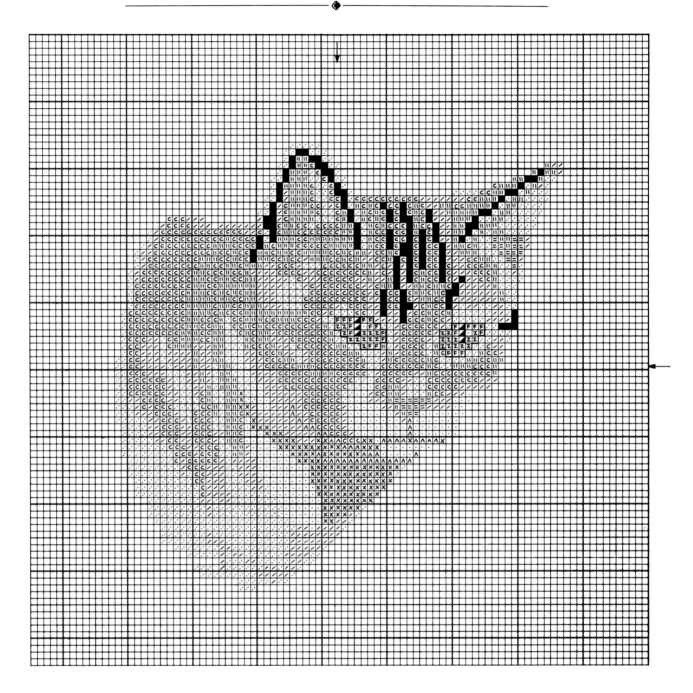

	420 dark hazelnut brown	△	318 light steel grey	◪	310 black and outline eyes
‖	680 dark old gold	✕	415 pale grey	═	754 light peach
∴	677 very light old gold	F	471 light avocado green	◨	676 light old gold
•	white	Z	472 very light avocado green	c	729 medium old gold

Surprise Encounter

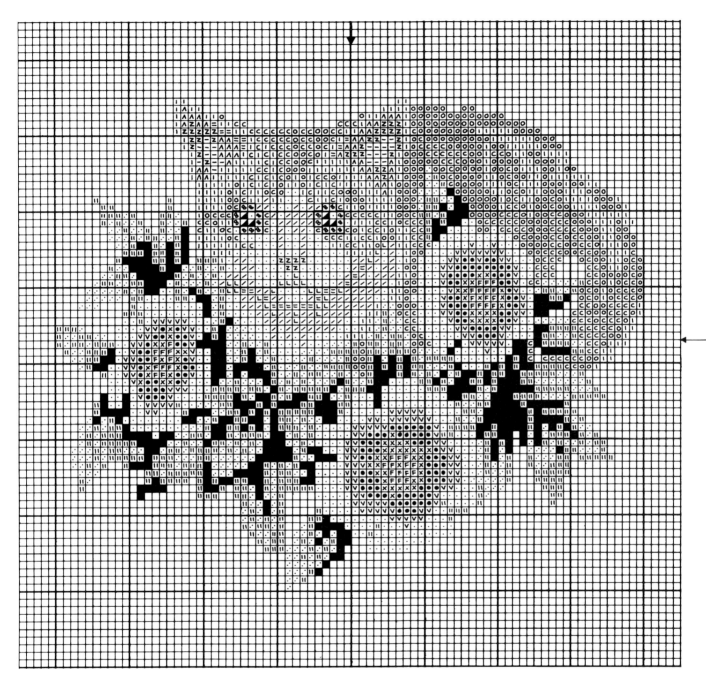

◤ 310	black and outline eyes	F 741	medium tangerine orange	Z 353	peach	C 839	dark beige brown
● 550	very dark violet	8 827	very light blue	■ 937	dark avocado green	O 3045	dark golden wheat
V 718	mulberry	L 318	light steel grey	‖ 470	medium avocado green	∧ 3064	spice brown
· white		= 414	steel grey	∴ 472	very light avocado green	⊟ 948	very light peach
× 307	lemon yellow	╱ 415	pale grey	I 3047	pale golden wheat		

Ginger Tom up a Tree

◆

◪ 640 dark beige grey	⊪ 676 light old gold
⌃ 3031 very dark brown	◹ 680 dark old gold
7 472 very light avocado green	◉ 729 medium old gold
· white	◸ 898 very dark coffee brown
× 504 light blue green	▤ 782 medium topaz brown
Ⅱ 677 very light old gold	613 light drab brown
■ 310 black	3 435 very light brown
● 414 steel grey	◺ 436 tan brown
L 3346 dark yellow green	◪ 433 medium brown
V 415 pale grey	2 611 dark drab brown
4 224 antique pink	8 829 dark avocado leaf brown
C 318 light steel grey	◁ 3045 dark golden wheat
T 434 light brown	+ 831 light avocado leaf brown

Expectation

- ● 367 dark pistachio green
- Z 368 light pistachio green
- X 320 medium pistachio green
- / 402 very light mahogany brown
- V 976 medium golden brown
- O 301 medium mahogany brown
- ■ 310 black and outline eyes
- · white
- Λ 317 medium steel grey
- 7 754 light peach
- C 451 shell grey
- ⁚ 453 light shell grey
- ◢ 726 light topaz yellow
- I 794 pale blue
- — 792 medium royal blue
- □ 414 steel grey
- II 415 pale grey
- = 762 very light pearl grey
- T 3348 light yellow green

EXPECTATION

Black-and-white Cat
with Pansies

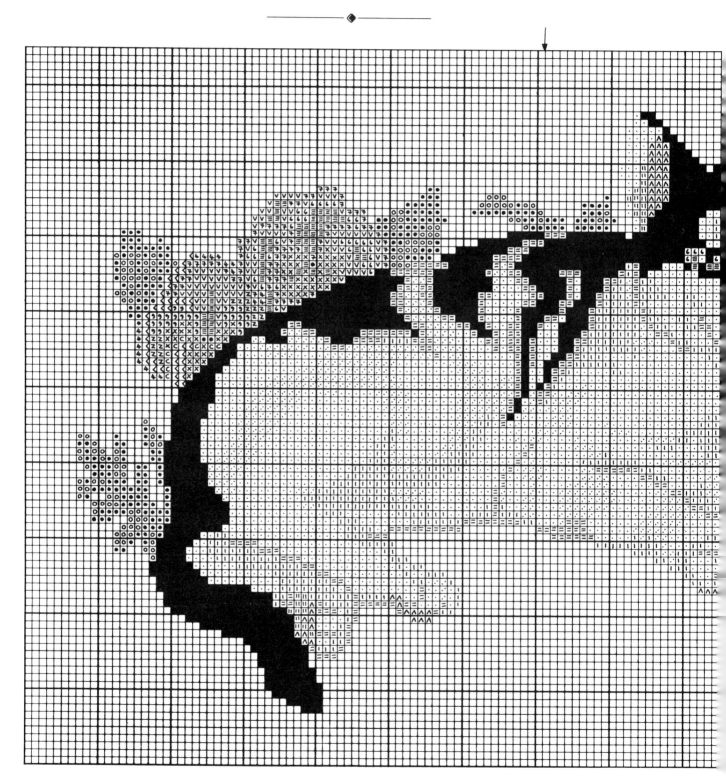

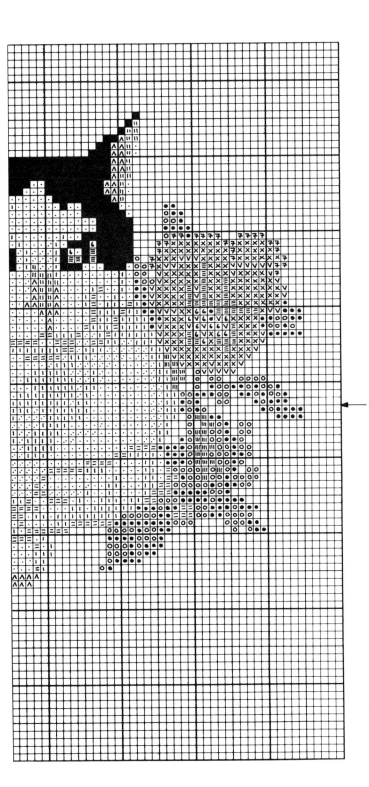

Z	3687 mauve
ꝯ	335 dark pink
●	3347 medium yellow green
○	3348 light yellow green
⫴	3346 dark yellow green
×	300 very dark mahogany brown
≣	743 dark yellow
V	977 golden brown
Ƚ	742 light tangerine orange
₮	976 medium golden brown
■	310 black
∧	758 pale brick red
‖	950 light antique pink
·	white
=	318 light steel grey
I	415 pale grey
∴	762 very light pearl grey
c	745 light yellow
⌐	315 dark antique mauve
◁	221 claret

Photo on p. 72

BLACK-AND-WHITE CAT WITH PANSIES
See pp.70–1

· OPPOSITE ·
BRITISH BI-COLOUR CAT
See pp.74–5

British Bi-colour Cat

⬤ 310 black and outline eyes, legs and paws

· white

⬚ 762 very light pearl grey

◿ 415 pale grey

◣ 318 light steel grey

|| 948 very light peach

☒ 353 peach

◯ 472 very light avocado green

Photo on p. 73

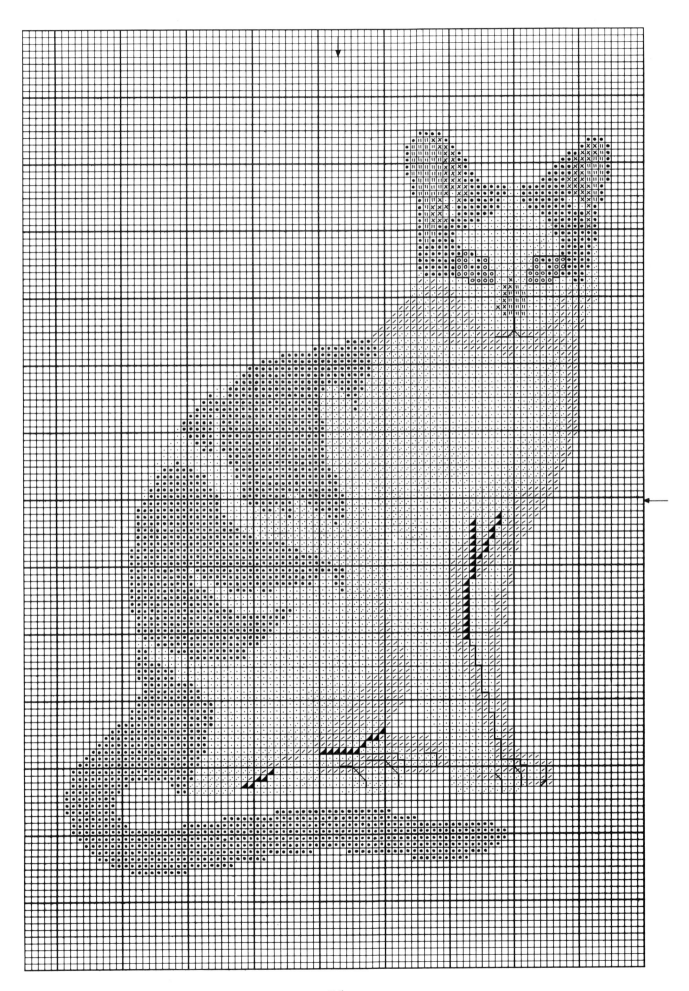

Long-haired Cat Sleeping amongst the Flowers

· white	⊟ 909 very dark emerald green	⧄ 3046 golden wheat
● 3685 dark mauve	■ 3031 very dark brown	⊔ 3045 dark golden wheat
⊠ 3687 mauve	‖ 830 avocado leaf brown	2 613 light drab brown
∧ 3688 medium mauve	⣀ 677 very light old gold	7 834 light golden wheat yellow
⊙ 954 nile green	∨ 832 golden wheat yellow	⊓ 3047 pale golden wheat
⊡ 912 light emerald green	⊏ 831 light avocado leaf brown	

LONG-HAIRED CAT SLEEPING
AMONGST THE FLOWERS

White Cat Waiting Hopefully

---◆---

- ☑ 353 peach
- ⊡ 948 very light peach
- ■ 310 black and outline eyes
- ☒ 3348 light yellow green
- ⊡ white
- ◉ 414 steel grey
- ◎ 415 pale grey
- ⊘ 762 very light pearl grey

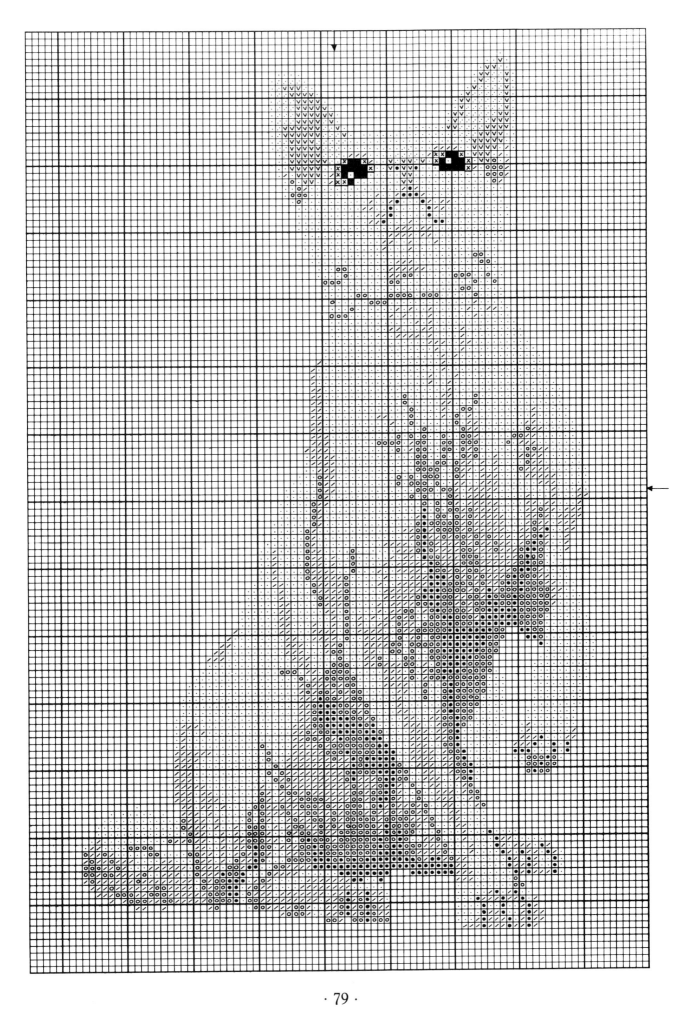

Long-haired Grey Kitten with Flowers

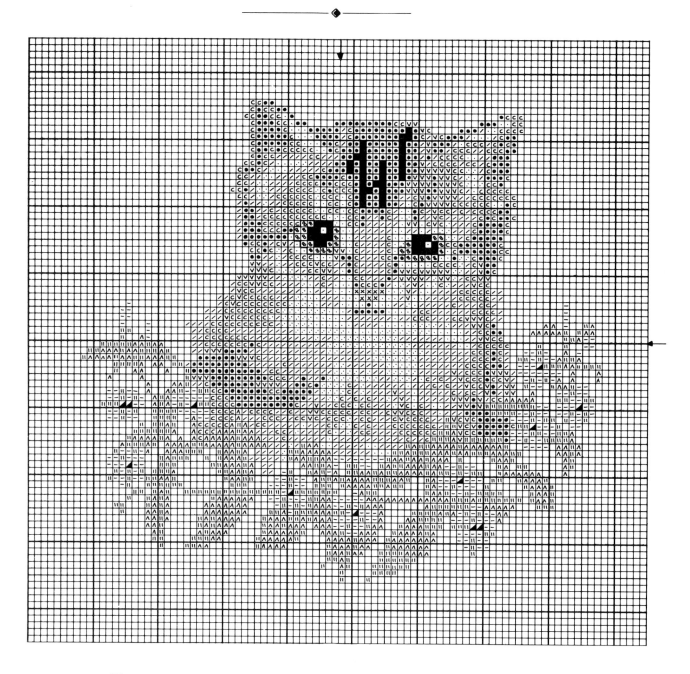

■ 310 black and outline eyes	⊘ 415 pale grey	⊟ 350 light red	
● 317 medium steel grey	C 318 light steel grey	◣ 743 dark yellow	
· white	V 414 steel grey	Λ 3348 light yellow green	
✕ 758 pale brick red	8 800 pale delft blue	‖ 3346 dark yellow green	
⸱ 762 very light pearl grey			

Ginger-and-white Long-hair

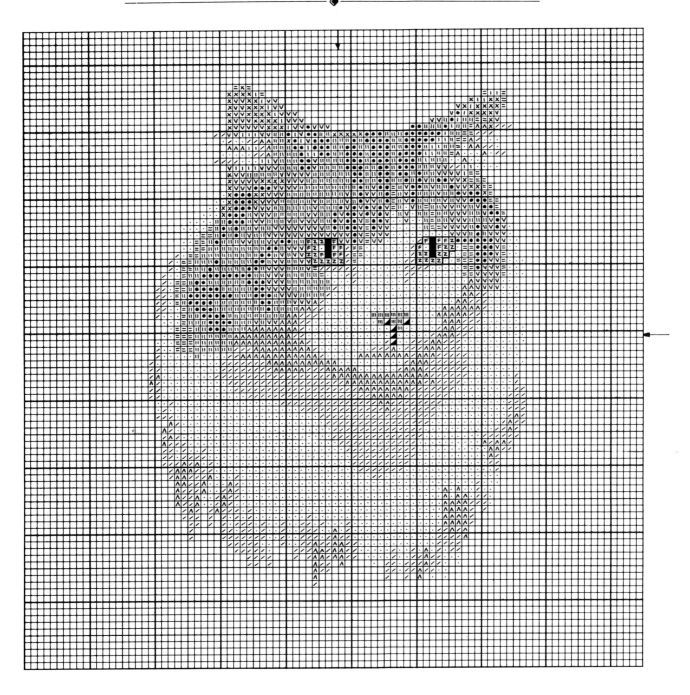

■	310	black and outline eyes	Ⅱ	830	avocado leaf brown	Ⅲ	754	light peach
·		white	✕	680	dark old gold	◢	352	medium peach
F	471	light avocado green	∨	729	medium old gold	╱	415	pale grey
Z	472	very light avocado green	=	676	light old gold	∧	414	steel grey
●	400	dark mahogany brown	Ⅰ	677	very light old gold			

Ginger-and-white Cat
on a Quilt

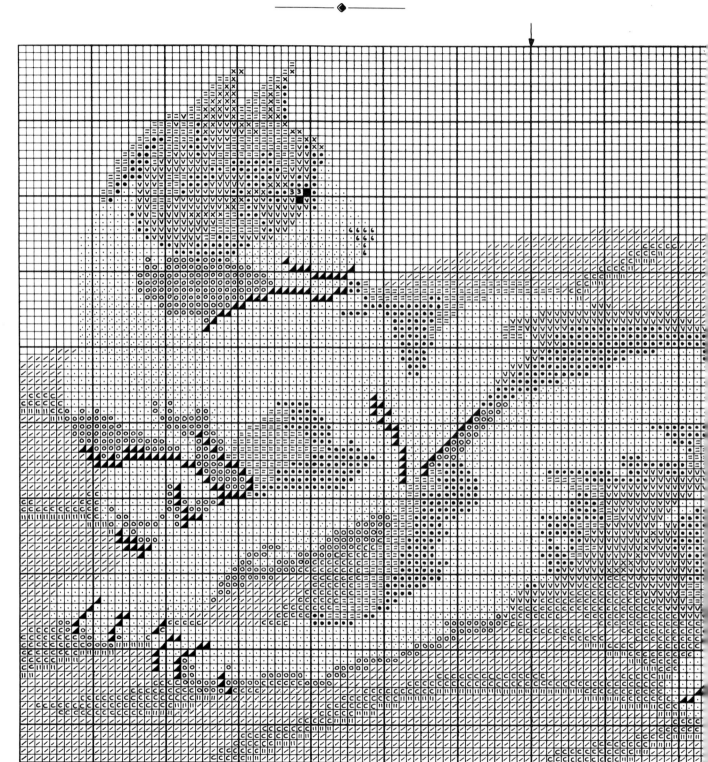

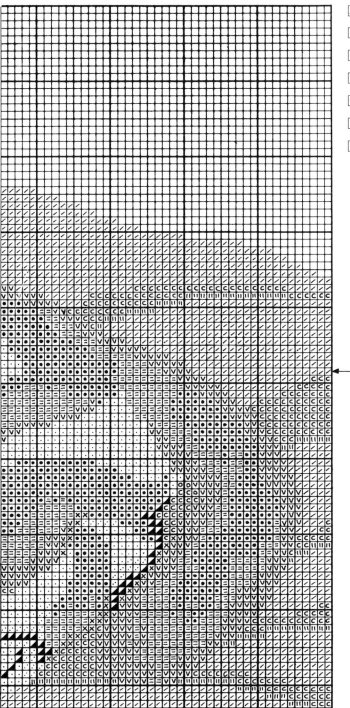

⧄	809	delft blue		⊡	822	light beige grey
Ⅱ	820	very dark royal blue		⊙	644	medium beige grey
c	798	dark delft blue		◪	640	dark beige grey
●	676	light old gold		·		white
☰	783	christmas gold		■	310	black
v	782	medium topaz brown		③	471	light avocado green
✕	780	very dark topaz brown		◖	353	peach

Photo on pp. 84–5

GINGER-AND-WHITE CAT
ON A QUILT
See pp.82–3

Cream Persian with Flowers

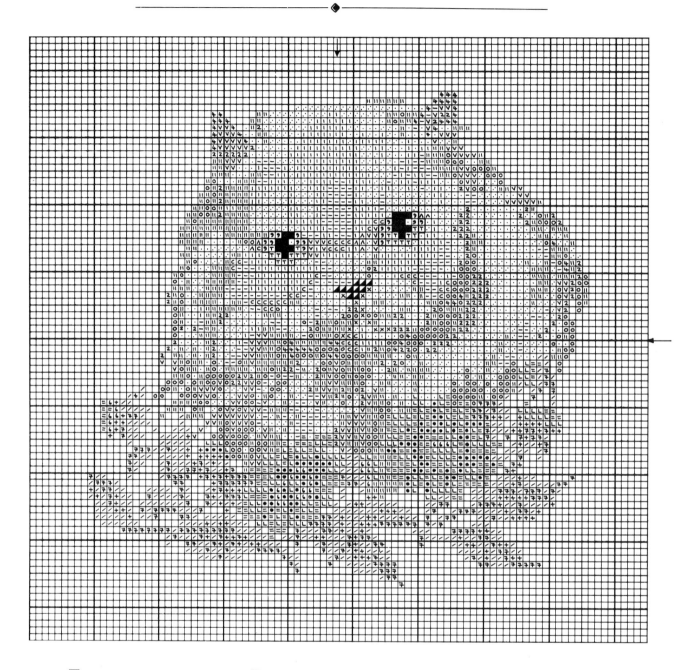

· white	☒ 762 very light pearl grey	ᴄ 725 topaz yellow
⋰ 951 very light apricot	◪ 758 pale brick red	＝ 977 golden brown
Ⅱ 945 light apricot	☒ 632 chocolate brown	● 975 dark golden brown
■ 310 black and outline eyes	─ 453 light shell grey	ʟ 976 medium golden brown
⊙ 318 light steel grey	c 452 medium shell grey	＋ 955 light nile green
‖ 415 pale grey	∧ 451 shell grey	╱ 989 light forest green
∨ 414 steel grey	т 402 very light mahogany brown	⁊ 987 dark forest green
⌴ 317 medium steel grey	⁊ 301 medium mahogany brown	

Sleeping Tabby

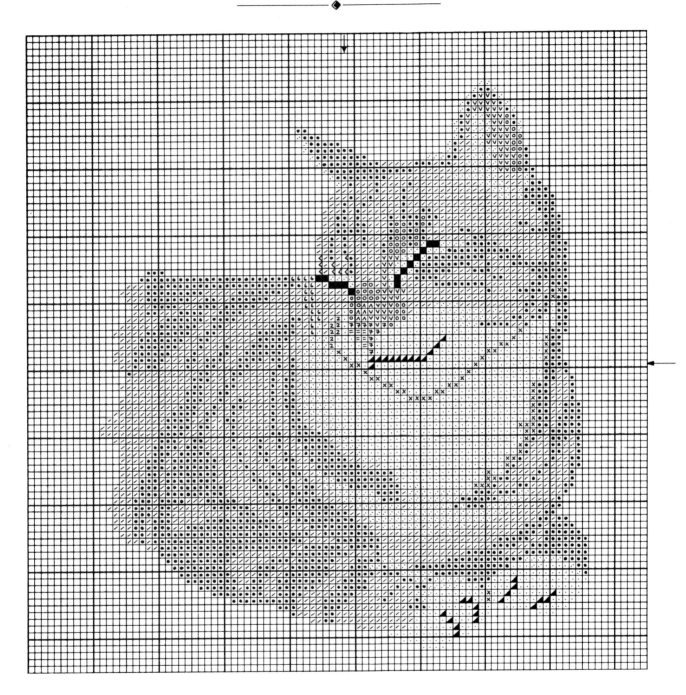

●	3031 very dark brown	⸪ 676 light old gold	∧	977 golden brown
■	310 black	⊘ 831 light avocado leaf brown	○	680 dark old gold
⊠	415 pale grey	↖ 610 very dark drab brown	⊰	729 medium old gold
◪	318 light steel grey	⊞ 645 dark beaver grey	⊡	677 very light old gold
⊡	white	≡ 758 pale brick red	⌄	829 dark avocado leaf brown

Photo on p. 88

SLEEPING TABBY
See p.87

· OPPOSITE ·

BLACK-AND-WHITE CAT WITH
FRENCH MARIGOLDS
See pp.90–1

Black-and-white Cat with French Marigolds

◆

⊡	754 light peach		◉	310 black
C	3064 spice brown		·	white
F	353 peach		☒	977 golden brown
■	317 medium steel grey		◖	975 dark golden brown
2	318 light steel grey		4	742 light tangerine orange
◿	415 pale grey		Ⅰ	726 light topaz yellow
◣	844 very dark beaver grey		⋁	989 light forest green
∧	647 medium beaver grey		⊙	987 dark forest green
⹀	646 beaver grey		T	725 topaz yellow
∓	648 light beaver grey		Ⅲ	783 christmas gold
L	645 dark beaver grey			

Photo on p. 89

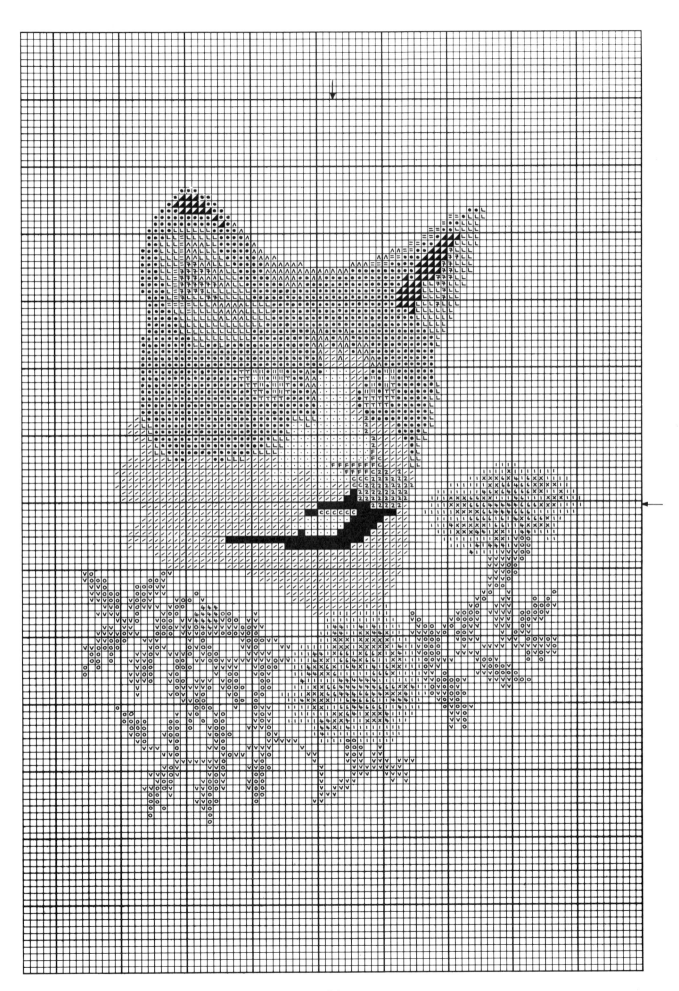

Blue Point Siamese with Flowers

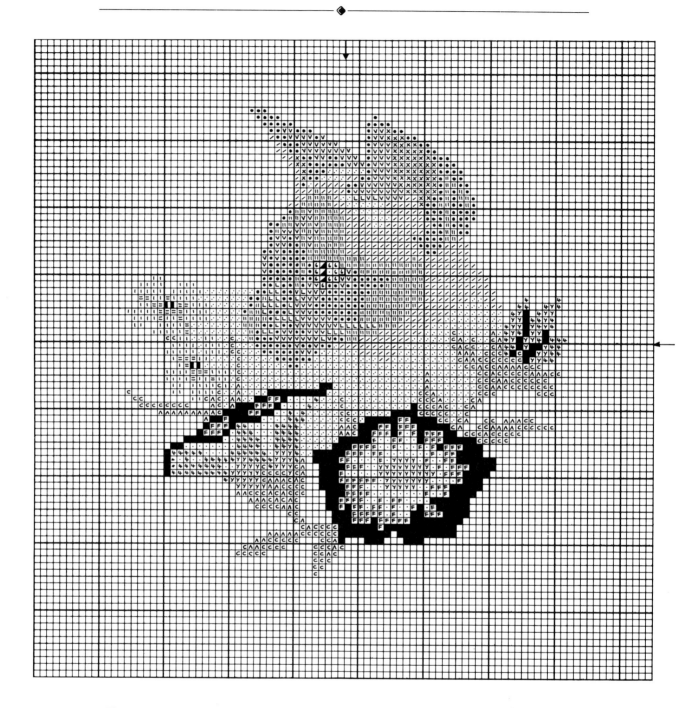

⊡	352 medium peach	⁴ 554 light violet	◪	310 black and outline eye
⊟	350 light red	ⓨ 744 medium yellow	⊡	ecru
■	221 claret	■ 550 very dark violet	⊘	842 very light beige brown
∧	368 light pistachio green	‖ 318 light steel grey	◙	413 very dark steel grey
ⓒ	367 dark pistachio green	⌊ 415 pale grey	⊠	451 shell grey
⒡	553 medium violet	⸨ 334 medium baby blue	⊻	414 steel grey
⊡	white			

BLUE POINT SIAMESE WITH FLOWERS

Waiting Patiently

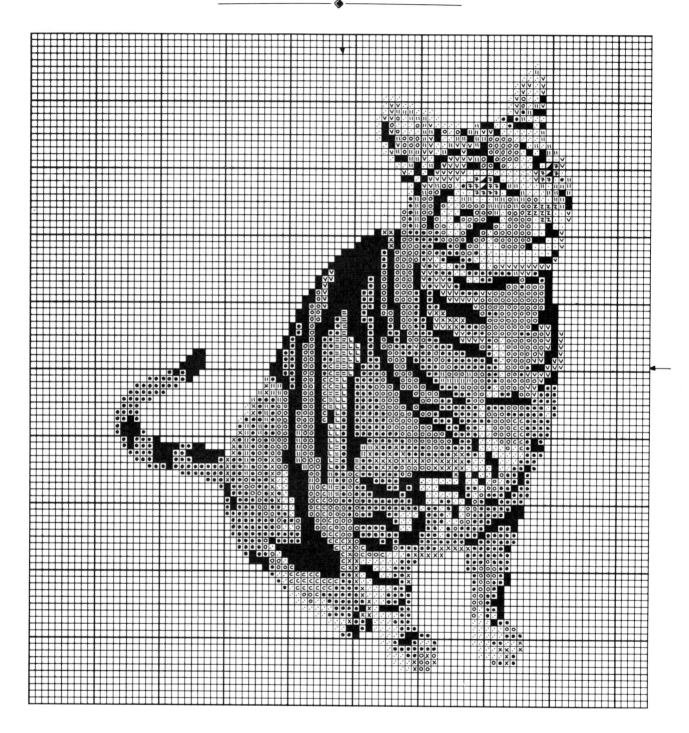

■	3031 very dark brown	☒ 610 very dark drab brown	Ⅱ 729 medium old gold
·	white	ⓒ 612 drab brown	L 738 very light tan
◪	310 black and outline eyes	⋮ 677 very light old gold	= 437 light tan brown
ꟻ	3348 light yellow green	⊙ 676 light old gold	Z 353 peach
●	611 dark drab brown	ⱽ 680 dark old gold	

Brown Tabby

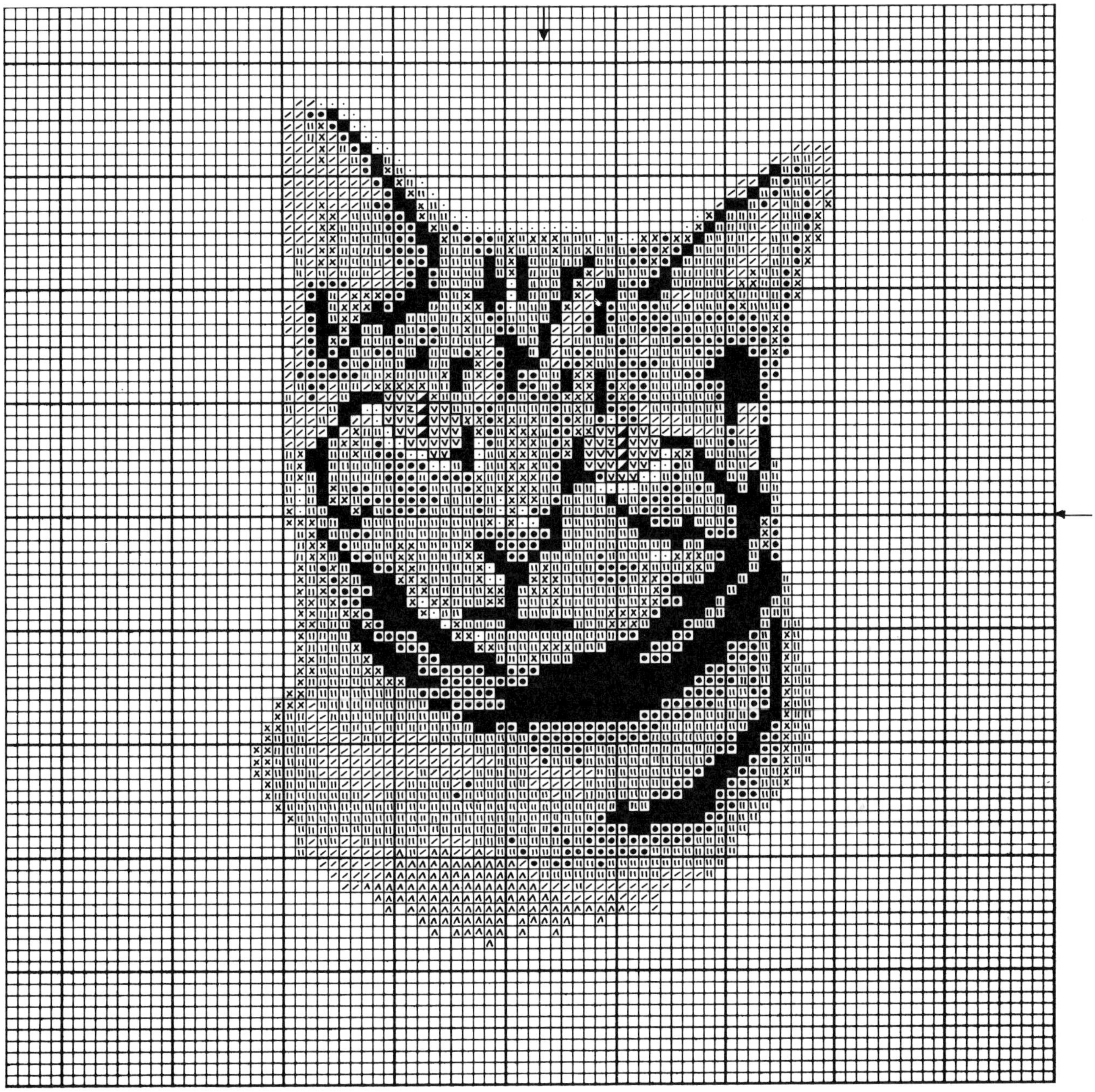

■ 3031 very dark brown and outline eyes	● 640 dark beige grey
^ 3047 pale golden wheat	/ 422 golden beige
· 822 light beige grey	◢ 310 black
× 644 medium beige grey	V 3348 light yellow green
‖ 642 beige grey	Z white